THE BATTLE OF ANTIETAM

ESSENTIAL LIBRARY OF
★THE CIVIL★
WAR

Essential Library

An Imprint of Abdo Publishing
abdopublishing.com

BY TOM STREISSGUTH

CONTENT CONSULTANT

ERIK B. ALEXANDER
ASSISTANT PROFESSOR
SOUTHERN ILLINOIS UNIVERSITY EDWARDSVILLE

abdopublishing.com

Published by Abdo Publishing, a division of ABDO, PO Box 398166, Minneapolis, Minnesota 55439. Copyright © 2017 by Abdo Consulting Group, Inc. International copyrights reserved in all countries. No part of this book may be reproduced in any form without written permission from the publisher. Essential Library™ is a trademark and logo of Abdo Publishing.

Printed in the United States of America, North Mankato, Minnesota

052016
092016

 THIS BOOK CONTAINS
RECYCLED MATERIALS

Cover Photo: Library of Congress
Interior Photos: Library of Congress, 1; Kurz & Allison/Library of Congress, 4; Rainer Lesniewski/Shutterstock Images, 8; Library of Congress, 10, 16, 23, 28, 34, 53; Corbis, 15, 19, 37, 38, 46, 57, 99 (right); Medford Historical Society Collection/Corbis, 12, 31; SuperStock/Glow Images, 21, 98 (top); The Print Collector/Heritage Images/Glow Images, 25; Brady National Photographic Art Gallery/Library of Congress, 44, 92; US National Archives and Records Administration, 41, 81; James Gardner/Library of Congress, 50; Timothy H. O'Sullivan/Bettmann/Corbis, 59; James Hope/National Park Service, 60, 74, 98 (bottom); Don Troiani/Corbis, 65, 83; iStockphoto, 68; Alexander Gardner/Library of Congress, 71, 87; Bettmann/Corbis, 63; Brady-Handy Photograph Collection/Library of Congress, 79; Alexander Gardner/Buyenlarge/Getty Images, 88; Hulton Archive/Getty Images, 95, 99 (left)

Editor: Arnold Ringstad
Series Designers: Kelsey Oseid and Maggie Villaume

Cataloging-in-Publication Data

Names: Streissguth, Tom, author.
Title: The Battle of Antietam / by Tom Streissguth.
Description: Minneapolis, MN : Abdo Publishing, [2017] | Series: Essential library of the Civil War | Includes bibliographical references and index.
Identifiers: LCCN 2015960300 | ISBN 9781680782721 (lib. bdg.) | ISBN 9781680774610 (ebook)
Subjects: LCSH: Antietam, Battle of, Md., 1862--Juvenile literature.
Classification: DDC 973.7/336--dc23
LC record available at http://lccn.loc.gov/2015960300

CONTENTS

CHAPTER 1   DUSK AT ANTIETAM CREEK 4

CHAPTER 2   THE CIVIL WAR ERUPTS 16

CHAPTER 3   TAKING THE WAR TO MARYLAND 28

CHAPTER 4   MARCHING TO ANTIETAM... 38

CHAPTER 5   THE EVE OF ANTIETAM 50

CHAPTER 6   THE DAY OF BATTLE 60

CHAPTER 7   FIGHTING AT THE ROHRBACH BRIDGE 74

CHAPTER 8   THE PROCLAMATION 88

TIMELINE 98
ESSENTIAL FACTS..100
GLOSSARY 102
ADDITIONAL RESOURCES....................................104
SOURCE NOTES 106
INDEX 110
ABOUT THE AUTHOR 112

In September 1862, the Battle of Antietam filled a field in rural Maryland with blood and smoke.

DUSK AT ANTIETAM CREEK

The dust of two great armies and the smoke of their rifles and cannons blanketed the fields lying west of Maryland's Antietam Creek. It was the late afternoon of September 17, 1862. Almost 12 hours of battle had left thousands of men dead and wounded. The Union and Confederate armies were at a stalemate. Neither side had gained much ground.

Outnumbered, the Confederate army of Northern Virginia was reeling from the heavy losses. Its commander, General Robert E. Lee, was holding Sharpsburg, Maryland, in a dangerous position. Only a few regiments protected the town. They faced much larger Union divisions to the east.

An attempt by Union troops to capture Sharpsburg might break Lee's army in two. The only escape route would take the Confederate forces to the banks of the Potomac River—and back to Virginia.

General George B. McClellan, commander of the Union army, faced a tough decision. He had several large units in reserve that he had kept out of the battle. In addition, batteries of Union artillery sat on the heights facing Sharpsburg. But an attack late in the day was risky. The dimming light would make it difficult for the Union gunners to spot their targets.

Although the Confederates were outnumbered, McClellan knew they could defend their position. Worse, they might counterattack and break through the Union lines. There were no Union regiments behind the lines that could stop an attack on the capital of Washington, DC, just 70 miles (110 km) to the east.

THE ROOTS OF THE WAR

The Battle of Antietam, also known as the Battle of Sharpsburg, was the bloodiest single day of the American Civil War (1861–1865). Several major battles had already taken place since the start of the conflict in April 1861. The Confederate armies had inflicted heavy defeats on the Union forces. But the battles had been fought in southern territory, leaving Union land relatively unscathed. The Union army still enjoyed an advantage in troops and resources.

The central issue of the war was the secession of 11 states from the country, and the expansion of the practice of slavery into newly admitted states in the West. The Confederate States of America, whose economy was based largely on slave labor, were claiming the right to exist as an independent country. The United States, under the leadership of President Abraham Lincoln, was fighting to restore the Union.

For many people in the South, the election of Abraham Lincoln in November 1860 threatened more than the expansion of slavery. As a result of the election, Lincoln's Republican Party captured both the presidency and a majority in Congress. That meant Southerners, who largely supported the Democratic Party, would now be in the minority. They feared the Northerners would trample on their rights, including perhaps the right to allow slavery within their borders.

THE MINORITY PRESIDENT

Abraham Lincoln's election as president was hotly opposed by a majority of Southerners, most of whom voted for the Democratic candidate. But the Democratic Party was deeply divided over the issue of slavery and put forward a Southern candidate, John Breckinridge, and a Northern one, Stephen Douglas of Illinois. With his opposition split, Lincoln won with a majority of the electoral votes but only approximately 40 percent of the popular vote.[1]

Lincoln favored banning slavery in new states and territories in the western frontier. He also favored sending freed slaves to colonies established in different regions of the world, including West Africa and the Caribbean.

BRITISH NORTH AMERICA

Oregon

Washington
Territory

Dakota Territory

Minnesota

Michigan

Wisconsin

New Hampshire
Vermont
Maine

Nevada
Territory

Utah
Territory

Nebraska Territory

Iowa

New York

Massachusetts

Rhode
Island
Connecticut

Pennsylvania

New Jersey

California

Colorado
Territory

Kansas

Illinois

Ohio

Indiana

Delaware
Maryland

Pacific

Missouri

Kentucky

West
Virginia

Virginia

BATTLE OF
ANTIETAM

Ocean

New Mexico
Territory

Indian
Territory

Arkansas

Tennessee

North Carolina

South
Carolina

Atlantic

Georgia

Texas

Alabama

Mississippi

Louisiana

Florida

Ocean

THE BAHAMAS

Union states without slavery

Union states and regions with slavery

Confederate states

Territories

MEXICO

Gulf of Mexico

The Battle of Antietam was fought near the border of the Union and the Confederacy.

Slaveholding states saw these policies as a threat. Banning slavery in new territories would damage the Southern economy, which depended on slave labor. Lincoln also believed that "compensated emancipation," or paying slave owners for their slaves' freedom, could gradually bring slavery to an end.[2] But slave owners in the South fiercely opposed this policy.

LINCOLN AND SLAVERY

Lincoln personally opposed slavery. But at the start of the Civil War, he was still willing to allow slavery to continue in those states where it was legal. Since the Constitution protected private property, including slaves, Lincoln believed the courts would strike down any law freeing the slaves as unconstitutional. Free and slaveholding states, in the president's opinion, should be able to reach a peaceful compromise on the question.

The debate between slave states and free states heated up in early 1861. Convinced the newly elected Lincoln would put their way of life at risk, leaders of several Southern states voted to secede from the Union. On February 9, these states established the Confederate States of America, with its capital at Montgomery, Alabama. As president, Lincoln believed his most important mission was to preserve the Union. At the outset of the war, his intention was to restore the Union whether or not it meant abolishing slavery.

The US Army was on a peacetime footing, and it was much too small to fight a war. Three days after a Confederate attack on Fort Sumter in South Carolina on April 12, Lincoln called for 75,000 volunteers to fight for the Union cause.[3] New regiments formed in New York, Massachusetts, and other Northern states.

The regular army issued the volunteers new uniforms and rifles. The authorities ordered them to Washington, DC, for training.

CONFLICTS IN MARYLAND

The establishment of the Confederate States of America split the country into three regions: North, South, and the four border states: Kentucky, Missouri, Delaware, and Maryland. Although Maryland had not joined the Confederacy, its laws allowed slavery. Many people in the state supported the Confederate cause. By a large majority, the citizens of the state's capital, Baltimore, voted against Abraham Lincoln and the Republican Party that had nominated him for the presidency.

Lincoln's views on the abolition of slavery evolved over the course of the war.

Maryland, like the rest of the nation, had its own regional divisions. In the eastern half of the state, tobacco farms relied on slave labor. In contrast, western Maryland was a region of steep hills, narrow creeks, forests, and small family farms. Slavery was nearly unknown in this half of the state. Western Marylanders were generally supportive of the Union cause.

In Maryland, the secession of Virginia on April 17, 1861, inspired proslavery factions to demand their state also join the Confederacy. Calls for a legislative vote on secession in Maryland prompted the governor to call a special session. But there were riots in Baltimore, and Union troops were occupying the key port of Annapolis. The lawmakers moved their proceedings to Frederick, a major city in western Maryland. On April 29, this body voted 53–13 against secession.[4]

TROUBLE IN SHARPSBURG

Antietam was not the only fighting in Maryland. The state was the scene of frequent conflict between proslavery and abolitionist factions. The Union army stationed troops in the area and patrolled the Potomac River to stop volunteers crossing the river to join the Confederates. Union troops also strained local hospitality, as eyewitness Angela Davis described:

At times we were not only surrounded by Union soldiers, but they were right in our midst, the stores being crowded with them; most of them wanted crackers and cheese, whiskey and tobacco, cigars and letter paper. . . . Often at midnight we were awakened by the rat-tat-tat of the drum, the shrill notes of the fife and the tramp, tramp of the men, followed by heavy baggage wagons; and would soon find that two or three regiments were passing through town.[5]

Many citizens of Baltimore resisted the presence of federal troops there.

Maryland would remain within the Union. But Governor Thomas Hicks also made a request to the federal government to no longer send or station troops in his state. The leaders of Maryland sought neutrality in the Civil War. They wanted to spare the state from any more political and military conflict. But they would soon be disappointed. In September 1862, the Civil War reached the peaceful hills of western Maryland.

THE TURNING POINT

Dusk was approaching the skies over Antietam Creek late on September 17. General McClellan rode out from his headquarters at the Pry farmhouse just east of Sharpsburg. His goal was to inspect IX Corps on his left flank. He knew Confederate reinforcements under General A. P. Hill were fighting with IX Corps. Reports said the Union troops were badly damaged and were retreating from the battlefield.

The Union commander could not be sure of the Confederate numbers, their exact position, or General Lee's intentions. Throughout the war, McClellan's habit was to overestimate the number of enemy troops his units were facing. At this crucial point of the battle, he was not sure whether to attack or order his commanders to stand their ground. The outcome of the entire war could be riding on his decision. Uncertain and hesitant, the general returned to his headquarters. He would order his army to stand its ground and wait for the morning to come.

DIVIDING UP THE ARMIES

The basic unit formation of the Civil War was the regiment, a unit of approximately 1,000 officers and men led in most cases by a colonel. Several regiments, sometimes with an attached artillery battery, made up a brigade. An army division was a larger unit including several brigades and one or more artillery batteries. Two or more divisions were grouped into a corps, the largest battlefield unit of the Civil War era.

During a campaign, regiments lost men to straggling, desertion, and illness. In most battles, including Antietam, the majority of regiments did not take part at full strength. It was also common for regiments, brigades, and divisions to be reformed or attached to other units when their numbers fell to much less than full strength.

Divisions were commonly reorganized and moved from one corps to another; IV Corps at Antietam, for example, consisted of a single division. IX Corps had four divisions as well as several unattached regiments.

Union forces at Antietam included I, II, IV, VI, IX, and XII Corps, as well as a single cavalry division consisting of five brigades. The Confederate army named its largest units after commanders. At Antietam, the Confederacy brought into battle McLaws's, Anderson's, Jackson's, Ewell's, D. H. Hill's, Jones's, Jenkins's, Walker's, Hood's, and A. P. Hill's divisions, as well as a separate artillery reserve under the command of Brigadier General William Pendleton.

One battery of the Second US Artillery Regiment of the Union XII Corps was photographed in Virginia in the summer of 1862.

The capital of the United States, Washington, DC, was only lightly defended at the outset of the war.

THE CIVIL WAR ERUPTS

The border state of Maryland did not join the Confederacy, but its laws allowed slavery, and many people in the state supported the Southern cause. One of Lincoln's key goals early in the war was to hold on to the border states, including Maryland. But as the Confederacy began to form, its leaders believed they could convince Maryland to join them.

This would leave Washington, DC, the federal capital, surrounded by hostile territory. Maryland lay to the north and Virginia to the south. If Maryland left the Union, the federal government might be forced to abandon the capital and move to Philadelphia, Pennsylvania, or New York City, New York. This would give the Confederates control of the US Capitol and the White House, as well as a string of forts that surrounded the city.

On the night of February 22, 1861, Lincoln boarded a train in Philadelphia. His destination was Washington, DC, where his inauguration as president was scheduled for the next day. The train would have to stop at the outskirts of Baltimore.

For Lincoln, this teeming port city was a dangerous place. Gangs of proslavery, anti-immigrant men known as Blood Tubs roamed the streets of Baltimore. They were known for intimidating voters on election days and dunking their opponents in vats of pigs' blood. When they heard Lincoln was passing through the city, the Blood Tubs plotted to kidnap or assassinate the president-elect.

Word of the plots reached Lincoln and his advisers. They planned to move the president-elect through the city in the dead of night. Baltimore banned the use of steam locomotives within the city limits. A team of horses would have to draw Lincoln's railcar through the streets.

Accompanied by a single bodyguard, Lincoln prepared for an attempt on his life. But that night the Blood Tubs failed to locate him. The president-elect arrived in Washington safely the next morning.

THE QUESTION OF SLAVERY

In the opinion of Lincoln, holding men and women as slaves was against the country's founding principles. But the Constitution did not directly address slavery. Although many Northern states banned slavery, in states where the practice was allowed, slaves were legal private property. They had no rights whatsoever. In a ruling known as the *Dred Scott* decision, issued by the US Supreme Court in 1857, African-American people could not be citizens. Further, an escaped slave had to be returned to his or her owner, even after reaching free territory.

Lincoln was a small-town lawyer from Illinois. He was familiar with legal decisions on slavery. Lincoln felt the free and slaveholding states should be able to reach a peaceful solution to the issue. He held to that belief even as the seceding states formed the Confederate States of America.

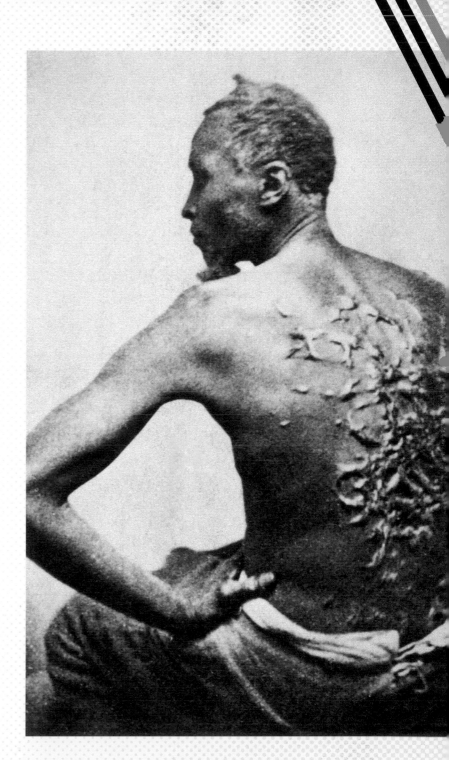

Slaves endured brutal conditions and punishments at the hands of their owners.

At this time, the regular US Army was not quite prepared for full-scale war with the Confederacy. Its highest-ranking officer was Lieutenant General Winfield Scott, a veteran of the Mexican-American War (1846–1848) and the War of 1812 (1812–1815). But Scott was 74 years old and so overweight he could no longer mount a horse. Scott searched the ranks for an able commander who could lead the Union forces into battle and defeat the Confederates.

THE WAR'S PURPOSE

In a letter to editor Horace Greeley of the *New York Tribune* just three weeks before the Battle of Antietam, Lincoln explained his ideas on slavery and secession:

> My paramount object in this struggle is to save the Union, and is not either to save or to destroy slavery. If I could save the Union without freeing any slave I would do it, and if I could save it by freeing all the slaves I would do it; and if I could save it by freeing some and leaving others alone I would also do that. What I do about slavery, and the colored race, I do because I believe it helps to save the Union; and what I forbear, I forbear because I do not believe it would help to save the Union.[1]

FIRING ON FORT SUMTER

In April 1861, the federal government still controlled four fortresses in Confederate territory. The most important was Fort Sumter. This massive structure lay on a small island in the harbor of Charleston, South Carolina—the first state to secede from the Union. Charleston was one of the Confederacy's key seaports, and Confederate leaders made capturing Fort Sumter their first military objective.

Fort Sumter endured many hours of cannon fire from Confederate forces along the shore.

On April 12, shore batteries in Charleston under the command of General P. G. T. Beauregard opened fire on the fort. Thousands of artillery rounds struck the walls and ramparts, but no one was killed. After two days of shelling, Major Robert Anderson, Sumter's Union commander, agreed to surrender the fort. Anderson ordered a final 50-gun salute, during which one cannon exploded and killed a Union soldier. The garrison then boarded small boats and escaped from Charleston Harbor. The Civil War had begun.

On April 15, Lincoln called for volunteers to form regiments in states still loyal to the Union. Brimming with excitement for the battles to come, the men of the Sixth Massachusetts gathered at Faneuil Hall in central Boston. They drilled in the streets and waited for orders to move out.

Union officials offered command of the US Army to Robert E. Lee of Virginia. Lee was a graduate of West Point, the army's military academy. He gained fighting experience during the Mexican-American War. He was considered by Scott and others to be one of the nation's finest commanders. But Lee felt a strong loyalty to his home state of Virginia.

Lincoln's call for volunteers angered Southern states that had not yet seceded. The leaders of these states, including Tennessee, wanted no part of fighting fellow Southerners. The leaders of Virginia refused to comply with the order to raise troops. On April 17, Virginia seceded from the Union and joined the Confederacy. Unwilling to fight his fellow Virginians, Lee decided against the offer. He resigned from the US Army and accepted an officer's commission in the Confederate army.

ROBERT E. LEE

1807–1870

Having fought valiantly for the US Army during the Mexican-American War, Robert E. Lee faced a hard decision as Virginia seceded from the Union in April 1861. Lee's loyalty to Virginia eventually overcame his lifelong professional commitment as an army officer. As he saw it, serving the Union cause would be a betrayal of his home state as well as his family.

The son of renowned Revolutionary War (1775–1783) cavalry officer Henry Lee, the general resigned his army commission on April 20 and became commander in chief of military forces defending Virginia. He was named commander of the Army of Northern Virginia in May 1862. During the Maryland campaign in September, Lee made the risky decision to split his forces before the Battle of Antietam. The result was a stalemate on the battlefield but a Confederate retreat from Maryland.

Lee led the rebels to victory at Fredericksburg and Chancellorsville, but was outfought at Gettysburg, where the Confederates were thrown back with heavy losses. Nevertheless, Lee kept the high regard of Confederate president Jefferson Davis, who stayed loyal to his leading general up to the time of Lee's surrender to General Ulysses S. Grant at Appomattox Court House in Virginia on April 9, 1865. The surrender ended the Civil War. After the war, Lee became the president of Washington College in Virginia. He died in October 1870.

THE BALTIMORE RIOT

For most Northern regiments, there was only one route to Washington. That route, like the president's, ran through Baltimore. On April 18, five companies of militia from Pennsylvania and an artillery unit from the regular army encountered a mob of angry, rock-throwing civilians at Baltimore's Bolton Street

WHY SECEDE?

In his speeches and writings, Confederate president Jefferson Davis made the case that the Civil War centered on the issue of slavery and the Northern efforts to restrict or abolish the practice:

> Fanatical organizations, supplied with money by voluntary subscriptions, were assiduously engaged in exciting amongst the slaves a spirit of discontent and revolt . . . the dogmas of these voluntary organizations soon obtained control of the Legislatures of many of the Northern States, and laws were passed providing for the punishment, by ruinous fines and long-continued imprisonment in jails and penitentiaries, of citizens of the Southern States who should dare to ask aid of the officers of the law for the recovery of their property. . . . Finally a great party was organized for the purpose of obtaining the administration of the Government, with the avowed object of using its power for the total exclusion of the slave States from all participation in the benefits of the public domain acquired by all the States in common, whether by conquest or purchase; of surrounding them entirely by States in which slavery should be prohibited; of thus rendering the property in slaves so insecure as to be comparatively worthless, and thereby annihilating in effect property worth thousands of millions of dollars.[2]

People in Baltimore lashed out violently at Union troops in the city.

RIGHTS IN WARTIME

The turmoil in Maryland led to drastic actions on the part of President Lincoln. After Maryland legislator John Merryman was arrested for hindering Union troops, his lawyer filed for a writ of habeas corpus. This allows the release of a prisoner so the charges against him or her can be heard in court. It is also a constitutional right: Article I, Section 9 of the Constitution declares "The privilege of the writ of habeas corpus shall not be suspended, unless when in cases of rebellion or invasion the public safety may require it."[4]

Believing current events threatened public safety and qualified as rebellion, Lincoln issued an emergency proclamation suspending habeas corpus in Maryland. Prisoners would remain prisoners as long as the government wished to hold them. The suspension of habeas corpus continued throughout the war.

station. The city's mayor, George Brown, then sent a warning to the president:

> *The people are exasperated to the highest degree by the passage of troops, and the citizens are universally decided in the opinion that no more should be ordered to come. It is my solemn duty to inform you that it is not possible for more soldiers to pass through Baltimore unless they fight their way at every step.*[3]

On the next day, the Sixth Massachusetts followed Lincoln to Baltimore. The volunteers arrived at the city limits and left their trains for horse-drawn wagons. The appearance of the Union troops provoked mobs in the city to attack with paving stones. A few of the local citizens also carried pistols. Shots rang out, and the regiment responded.

The mob and the Union troops traded jeers as bullets whistled off the pavement and buildings. Four men from the Sixth Massachusetts and 11 civilians were killed in the Baltimore Riot.[5] These were the first battle deaths of the Civil War.

A committee of Baltimore's leading citizens protested the movement of Union troops through the city. Lincoln replied, "Our men are not moles, and cannot dig under the earth. They are not birds, and cannot fly through the air. There is no way but to march across, and that they must do."[6] In response, pro-Confederate Marylanders cut telegraph lines and damaged railroad tracks and bridges linking the state to the city of Washington, DC. These actions were among the first conflicts in Maryland during the Civil War. But much worse was yet to come.

By the war's end, much of Richmond, Virginia, would lay in ruins.

TAKING THE WAR TO MARYLAND

To many in the Confederacy, the North had become a hostile foreign power, Lincoln was a tyrant, and the Republican-led Congress posed a threat to the practice of slavery. The Confederate States of America moved their capital to Richmond, Virginia, just 100 miles (160 km) from Washington, DC. The Confederate government appointed Jefferson Davis, a US senator, military veteran, and planter from Mississippi, as their president. For Davis, the goal of the Civil War was to maintain the practice of slavery in a new, independent nation. Davis and other Southern leaders agreed on their strategy. They would attempt to hold their ground, defend their cities, and convince the US government to leave them alone.

THE NORTHERN STRATEGY

The federal capital of Washington, DC, was in a precarious geographic position. It lay on the north bank of the Potomac River between Maryland and the state of Virginia. Virginia was home to the Confederate capital of Richmond. Only a few days' march separated the two cities. Washington, DC, was protected by strong fortifications, but could be surrounded and cut off from the rest of Union territory if a Confederate army crossed the Potomac and invaded Maryland.

The regular US Army was much too small to undertake an offensive against Confederate territory. For that reason, in early 1861, the largest Union force in the east, the Army of the Potomac, trained new volunteer regiments.

Lincoln believed there was still a chance to reconcile the country by appealing to moderates, nonslaveholders, and Unionists in the South. He also knew the federal army was not prepared for an outright invasion of the Confederate homeland. He wanted to avoid a destructive war. Instead, he agreed to assaults along the South's edges: in the west along the Mississippi Valley, in northern Virginia, and along the Outer Banks of North Carolina. In addition, the Union imposed a maritime blockade, intended to cut the South off from its export markets in Europe. If it could capture New Orleans, Louisiana, the North could rob the South of its most important seaport and one of its largest cities.

Union troops drilled and trained in the field as they prepared for battle.

MCCLELLAN TAKES THE REINS

The early months of the war went well for the Confederacy. On July 21, Southern armies earned a victory at Manassas, Virginia, in the Battle of Bull Run. After the fight, panicked Union armies retreated to Alexandria, Virginia, on the southern bank of the Potomac River. Southerners believed Bull Run proved they had the superior army. They thought the war would soon be over.

Lincoln demoted General Irvin McDowell, leader of the Union armies at Bull Run, and appointed General George McClellan as overall commander of the Union armies defending Washington, DC. McClellan was a master of military

NAMING BATTLES

The Union and Confederate commanders had different ways of naming their battles. For the Confederate army, battles were customarily named after nearby towns. On the Union side, natural features such as mountains or rivers were more important. As a result, many Civil War battles carry two names. The First and Second Battles of Bull Run, for example, are still widely referred to among Southerners as First and Second Manassas. The Battle of Antietam is also known as the Battle of Sharpsburg.

training and logistics. His energy and charisma made him popular among the public and the men under his command. McClellan's appointment fueled his ambition to become a national leader. In a letter to his wife, he wrote:

> I find myself in a new & strange position here—Presdt, Cabinet, Genl Winfield Scott & all deferring to me—by some strange operation of magic I seem to have become the power of the land. I almost think that were I to win some small success now I could become Dictator or anything else that might please me—but nothing of that kind would please me—I won't be Dictator.[1]

Earlier in the year, McClellan had led Union armies that drove Confederate forces out of western Virginia. McClellan announced that slave owners in the region could keep their legal property. But people in this region, although they were citizens of a Confederate state, generally opposed secession.

After McClellan's campaign they began working to separate from Virginia. Their effort succeeded in 1863 with the establishment of West Virginia.

McClellan was a cautious military commander. He avoided battle unless his armies held a strong advantage in numbers and position. He often overestimated the size and power of his opposition. After the battle of Bull Run, he spent several months drilling the Army of the Potomac and holding parades in Washington, DC. Although a Confederate army still held Manassas, McClellan would not launch an attack against it.

As the war continued, McClellan would also differ with Lincoln's decisions and approach to the war. Slavery, for him, was a minor issue and one not worth fighting for. "I am fighting to preserve the integrity of the Union," McClellan wrote in a letter in November 1861. "To gain that end we cannot afford to raise up the negro question."[2]

A PLAN OF ATTACK

Winter came, and heavy rains turned the Virginia roads to mud. Confederate and Union armies remained in place. In the meantime, General McClellan drew up plans for an attack on Richmond. He would float his army down the Potomac River on a fleet of transport vessels. The army would land on the banks of the Rappahannock River, near the Confederate capital. The Army of the Potomac

GEORGE B. MCCLELLAN

1826–1885

The son of a well-off Philadelphia family, George B. McClellan believed from a young age he was destined for greatness. A capable soldier and charismatic officer, he earned the admiration of soldiers and civilians in the early months of the Civil War. But in leading the Army of the Potomac, McClellan also displayed a cautious, hesitant strategy that exasperated President Lincoln and drew the ridicule of Union newspapers. At one point, Lincoln quipped, "If General McClellan does not want to use the army, I should like to borrow it for a time."[3] This famous remark further damaged McClellan's opinion of Lincoln, whom he saw as nothing more than a small-town lawyer unsuited for national leadership.

When McClellan failed to pursue the Confederate army after Antietam, it was the last straw for Lincoln, who relieved the general of his command and replaced him with Ambrose Burnside. Sure that he knew better than Burnside or Lincoln how to lead an army, as well as a country, McClellan ran for president in 1864 and won the nomination of the Democratic Party. But in the November 8, 1864, election, the country fell in line behind Lincoln and the Republicans. McClellan captured 45 percent of the vote, winning only Kentucky, Delaware, and New Jersey, at the time his home state.[4]

After the war, McClellan spent time as the president of a railroad. He served as the governor of New Jersey from 1878 to 1881. He later spent time traveling and writing his autobiography. McClellan died in October 1885.

would take the city by surprise and force the Confederate government to seek peace terms.

The campaign for Richmond began in the summer of 1862. It turned out badly for the Army of the Potomac. The Confederates put up a stout defense of Richmond and threw the Union armies back after the contentious Seven Days' Battle, fought between June 25 and July 1. Lincoln issued another proclamation, this time asking for another 300,000 volunteers to shore up the Union army.[5]

By this time, the president's patience with McClellan was running short. Lincoln believed McClellan's caution was costing time and lives. Lincoln also suspected McClellan was dragging out the war on purpose. By doing this, McClellan could accuse the administration of incompetence and boost his own chances to win the presidency.

The president and members of his cabinet knew General McClellan's personal hero was Napoleon Bonaparte, a brilliant French commander. In 1799, Napoleon had overthrown the French government in a military coup. He later proclaimed himself emperor, then conquered half of Europe at the head of the French army. In the newspapers, McClellan was often given the nickname "the Young Napoleon."[6]

PREPARING FOR A LONG WAR

After Bull Run and the Seven Days' Battle, Lincoln realized the war would endure longer than he had hoped. The Union required a total victory to end the Southern rebellion and the division of the country. This was the only path remaining to the abolition of slavery, which could not be achieved by negotiating with the Confederate government.

In the meantime, President Jefferson Davis appointed General Robert E. Lee as commander of the Confederate armies in Virginia. A brilliant strategist, Lee suggested an offensive against the Union armies holding central Virginia under General John Pope. Before the Union armies could regroup, he might have a chance to invade Maryland and strike Washington, DC.

For his part, Davis believed a decisive Confederate victory north of the Potomac River might convince the United Kingdom and France to side with the South. Lee prepared his army. It included several elite brigades as well as a renowned Confederate commander who would play a crucial role in the battles ahead: Thomas "Stonewall" Jackson.

Tensions between McClellan, *right*, and Lincoln were running high by late 1862.

Union and Confederate troops clashed repeatedly in Virginia in the late summer of 1862.

MARCHING TO ANTIETAM

After his defeat at the Seven Days' Battle, General McClellan retreated from southern Virginia. He brought his army back to Washington, DC, to regroup. In the meantime, the Confederate force under Robert E. Lee also moved north from Richmond. Their goal was to defeat another Union army, this one under the command of General John Pope. Lee wanted to act quickly, before McClellan had a chance to reinforce Pope.

Lee may not have realized Pope and McClellan were bitter rivals. Pope supported the abolition of slavery through the military conquest of the South. He favored a destructive, punishing war against the Confederacy and the seizure by force of enemy property, including slaves. McClellan simply wanted the Union restored, with slavery allowed as it had been before the war. Although the two men were fighting on the same side, McClellan saw a victory by Pope as a threat to his own interests.

Between August 28 and August 30, 1862, the Confederate army clashed with Pope's forces at the Second Battle of Bull Run. The two armies met in the same area where they fought at the First Battle of Bull Run, the first major battle of the war. At a critical point, McClellan held back his own army. They were camped only a few hours' marching distance from the battlefield. Without these reinforcements, Pope was defeated and thrown back to the outskirts of Washington, DC. The Confederate capital of Richmond remained secure.

LEE TAKES THE INITIATIVE

After the Confederate victory at the Second Battle of Bull Run, General Lee ordered his army to continue north to the banks of the Potomac River. He had General Thomas "Stonewall" Jackson bring his army north from the Shenandoah River valley of western Virginia. Jackson would be the first to lead Confederate troops across the Potomac into Maryland. The crossing began on September 4 at White's Ford and Point of Rocks, approximately 50 miles (80 km) north of Washington, DC.[1]

STONEWALL JACKSON

1824–1863

One of the most famous officers of the Civil War, Thomas "Stonewall" Jackson was, like many Union and Confederate generals, a graduate of the US Military Academy at West Point and a veteran of the Mexican-American War. After serving under Scott in Mexico, Jackson joined the faculty at the Virginia Military Institute in Lexington, Virginia. His students knew him as a strict but capable instructor with some odd personal quirks, such as holding his arm constantly above his head to compensate for what he believed was a physical defect.

Although he was opposed to the secession of Virginia, Jackson joined the Confederate army and proved a brilliant commander. He earned his famous nickname by leading a courageous charge at the First Battle of Bull Run. In the Shenandoah Valley of western Virginia, Jackson led his troops to several victories, forcing the Union forces to retreat from the valley. At Antietam, he held Lee's left wing against ferocious attacks by McClellan's troops. Later that year, in December, he also took part in a crucial Confederate victory at Fredericksburg. Jackson's luck ran out after the Battle of Chancellorsville, when he was mortally wounded by friendly fire from a North Carolina regiment. He died on May 10, 1863.

Lee now intended to bring the war to Union territory. His objective was a crucial railroad line that ran through Harrisburg, Pennsylvania. If the Confederates captured this junction, they would break an important Union supply line linking the eastern states with Ohio and the northwest. They could threaten Harrisburg as well as Baltimore and Washington, DC, which now lay south of the Confederate lines. A siege of Washington, DC, would be costly for both sides, but Lee believed it might force Lincoln to negotiate for peace.

Lee also believed Marylanders were sympathetic to the Confederacy. This border state allowed slavery, and Marylanders had volunteered for both Union and Confederate regiments. Lee believed he would be operating in friendly territory—a crucial advantage for any invading force. If they could win a major battle in Union-held territory, Lee and Jackson hoped they might be able to

HUNGRY, BAREFOOT, AND SICK

The toughest problem facing Civil War commanders on both sides was supply. During the Antietam campaign, Confederate soldiers were hungry; many went barefoot after wearing out their shoes. Alexander Hunter of Virginia described some of the harsh realities of the campaign:

On the 8th we struck up the refrain of "Maryland, My Maryland!" and camped in an apple orchard. We went hungry, for six days not a morsel of bread or meat had gone in our stomachs—and our menu consisted of apples and corn . . . Our under-clothes were foul and hanging in strips, our socks worn out, and half of the men were bare-footed, many were lame and were sent to the rear; others, of sterner stuff, hobbled along and managed to keep up, while gangs from every company went off in the surrounding country looking for food.[2]

persuade Maryland civilians to abandon their support for the Union and throw in with the Confederacy.

As part of this effort, Lee composed a proclamation to the people of Maryland:

> *The people of the Confederate states . . . have seen with profound indignation their sister State deprived of every right and reduced to the condition of a conquered province. We have long wished to aid you in throwing off this foreign yoke, to enable you again to enjoy the inalienable rights of freemen.*[3]

On the Union side, the defeat at the Second Battle of Bull Run cast a sense of foreboding over President Lincoln, his military leaders, and the members of his cabinet. The war would not be over quickly, as they had once hoped. McClellan had failed to capture Richmond, score a decisive victory against Lee, or reinforce another Union army during a critical battle. Dissension and rivalries among his commanders threatened Lincoln's goal of restoring the Union.

After the defeat at the Second Battle of Bull Run, Pope was relieved of his command and sent to an outpost in wintry Minnesota, on the distant northwest frontier. Although he was unhappy with General McClellan's actions during the Second Battle of Bull Run, Lincoln felt he had no choice. Only one of his top-ranking officers still enjoyed the undivided loyalty of the Union troops and widespread popularity among Northern civilians. The president asked George

McClellan to command the combined Union forces in the North and defeat Lee's invading Confederates.

MANEUVERS IN MARYLAND

For McClellan, the contest with Lee was personal. Lee and McClellan had both served as staff officers to General Scott during the Mexican-American War. Both men greatly respected Scott, but Lee had received the general's highest praise and had been promoted faster. In April 1861, Scott, as the head of the War Department, had offered Lee command of the Union armies. When Lee remained loyal to his home state of Virginia, Scott appointed Irvin McDowell commander of the Union troops at Washington, DC.

General Pope's loss at the Second Battle of Bull Run led to major changes in Union military leadership.

McClellan remained resentful and ambitious. He saw himself as a far superior commander to McDowell, and McDowell's defeat at Bull Run seemed to prove it. Above all, McClellan was determined to prove Scott wrong and raise himself, in the popular imagination, as the Union's supreme leader. In McClellan's view, Lincoln was nothing more than a simple country lawyer, and hardly presidential material. His own troops seemed to agree that McClellan was the best battlefield commander in the army.

At the moment, however, a more pressing problem was the Confederate army marching at will through western Maryland toward southern Pennsylvania. To deal with this threat, McClellan divided his army in three and moved it northwest from Washington, DC, to intercept the Confederates. One force held close to the Potomac River, while the others marched farther north, headed for the Maryland towns of Frederick and Hagerstown.

In the meantime, General Lee searched for an ideal location to battle the Union army. Civil War commanders carefully maneuvered their forces while out of enemy range. Their scouts and cavalry pickets surveyed the ground while staff officers pored over detailed maps. They sought elevated ground for their artillery, dense forests from which to mount surprise attacks, and waterways to serve as barriers to enemy advances.

Western Maryland had all three features in abundance. High spurs of the Allegheny Mountains crossed the region from north and south. In the plains

Small picket forces on each side stood guard to offer early warning of enemy actions.

and valleys, small farms lay among forests and tributaries flowing south to the Potomac.

The Confederates still had a serious problem along their supply lines back to western Virginia. Lee had expected his invasion of Maryland would convince the Union commanders at Harpers Ferry and Martinsburg in northwestern Virginia to retreat. However, the Union commanders held their ground. The garrisons together could muster 13,000 troops. They could easily block any Confederate retreat, cut the Confederate supply lines into Maryland, or even attack Lee from the rear.

To deal with this threat, Lee ordered three separate detachments under Generals Jackson, Lafayette McLaws, and John Walker to approach Harpers Ferry from the west, north, and east, respectively. Their mission was to surround the town, force the Union commander to surrender, and return to Maryland as quickly as possible to rejoin the main Confederate force.

The mission would take time. Harpers Ferry sat at the junction of the Potomac and Shenandoah Rivers. The town was surrounded by steep elevations, including Bolivar Heights to the west and Maryland Heights to the north across the Potomac. To capture the town, the Confederates would have to seize and hold these hills.

GENERAL LEE AT HARPERS FERRY

The 1862 Maryland campaign was not the first time Lee encountered an opponent at Harpers Ferry, Virginia. In October 1859, an antislavery leader named John Brown had staged a raid on the federal arsenal there. Brown's goal was to set off a nationwide slave uprising that would spread throughout the South and decide the issue once and for all.

Brown and his followers were able to fight their way into Harpers Ferry and seize the arsenal's engine house building. A detachment of US Marines quickly rushed to the scene. Their mission was to capture or kill Brown, and their leader was Colonel Lee. The Marines stormed the engine house and captured Brown. He was later hanged for treason. Lee's success inspired Lincoln and Scott to offer him command of the Union army in 1861.

They would have to avoid costly, time-consuming street fighting and lay down an artillery barrage heavy enough to force the Union commander to surrender. Jackson, McLaws, and Walker moved out on September 10.

SPECIAL ORDER 191

On September 13, Union soldiers discovered a small parcel lying on the littered ground of an abandoned Confederate camp near Frederick, Maryland. The small envelope had been opened; inside were several sheets of paper, used to wrap a bundle of three cigars. Pulling the sheets loose, the soldiers discovered a copy of Special Order 191—Lee's instructions to his generals for maneuvers in Maryland and the assault on Harpers Ferry.

THE MYSTERY OF THE LOST ORDER

General Lee's staff officer R. H. Chilton hurried to write out a copy of Special Order 191. A courier was dispatched with the order, which should have been sealed in its envelope. However, when Union troops discovered the order, it was unsealed, casually wrapped around three cigars.

Who lost the Lost Order? Was it dropped, or read and forgotten? The copy found by Union troops was meant for General D. H. Hill, who insisted he never received it. Chilton could not remember the name of the courier assigned to carry it. This person never came forward to admit his part in the events. Nobody on the Confederate side ever confessed to losing the order. Historians have not yet been able to sort out the mystery. The original Lost Order is now displayed in the US National Archives.

Within a few hours, Special Order 191 was in McClellan's hands. The Union commander realized Lee had divided his forces and would be seriously outnumbered in western Maryland for at least a day—longer if Harpers Ferry could hold out. At his headquarters, McClellan remarked to his staff: "Here is a paper with which, if I cannot whip Bobby Lee, I will be willing to go home."[4]

Lee had taken a very big risk. If McClellan could now concentrate his force against the Confederates in Maryland, he would have superior numbers and the battlefield advantage. But the window of opportunity would not remain open for long. McClellan would have to map out his strategy, issue orders, and move his troops into place quickly.

Scouts traveled on horseback into the dangerous, unpredictable areas between opposing armies.

THE EVE OF ANTIETAM

The fog of war made crucial decisions tough for Civil War generals. Their toughest foe was the confusion caused by dozens of reports from their own scouts, no two of which ever seemed to agree on the enemy's position or numbers. To further confuse the situation, officers on both sides sent out small cavalry units to skirmish with enemy scouts. When effective, these cavalry screens created uncertainty and hesitation on the part of opposing commanders.

After the discovery of Special Order 191, General McClellan ordered a reconnaissance of the Confederate lines to his west. His scouts brought back reports that a large force was maneuvering west of South Mountain. This ridge of thickly wooded land lay between McClellan's army and the town of Boonsboro, Maryland, where Lee had gathered his forces.

From the Lost Order, McClellan knew Lee had divided his force to attack Harpers Ferry. McClellan still estimated the Confederate army he was facing numbered more than 100,000 men—much larger than his own force. His estimate was, as usual, too high; Lee only had approximately 25,000 effective troops under his direct command, with the rest on their way to Martinsburg and Harpers Ferry.[1]

McClellan hesitated nearly a full day. Owing largely to his mistaken estimates of enemy forces, he could be a timid commander whose major objective was only to avoid defeat. McClellan knew Lee and his army must be driven back across the Potomac. But he also realized that if he lost the battle that was sure to come, the Confederate army would have a clear path to Washington, DC.

THE BATTLE OF SOUTH MOUNTAIN

After considering his scouts' reports, McClellan ordered his army forward to South Mountain on September 14. Their orders were to attack along the three narrow roads that crossed the mountain and to drive the Confederates back. The Union I Corps and IX Corps would advance on Turner's Gap at the top of the ridge, while General William Franklin's VI Corps would head for Crampton's Gap to the south. General Jacob Cox would lead a division against Fox's Gap, to the north of Turner's Gap. McClellan's orders were for VI Corps to capture

Though hundreds of men on both sides died during the Battle of South Mountain, it was a relatively minor skirmish compared to the coming clash at Antietam.

Crampton's Gap, push back the Confederates holding it, then turn farther south to advance on McLaws's forces and relieve the Union garrison at Harpers Ferry.

The narrow gaps at the top of South Mountain, however, would be easy for the Confederates to defend. The trees and underbrush on either side of the roads provided good cover, and any force coming along the roads would have to form a narrow file, making the soldiers easy targets for snipers. The rebels took up positions in the dense forest along the ridgeline and prepared to fire on the Union troops as they came up the eastern slopes.

Lee ordered General D. H. Hill and Jeb Stuart to defend the gaps. General James Longstreet would remain in reserve. If the Union forces broke through the defenses at the top of the hill, Longstreet would block their path forward. Lee would still have a clear route of retreat to the Potomac through the little town of Sharpsburg, near the north bank of the river. He could take up position around this town and prepare to defeat McClellan the next day.

SHARPSBURG, DC?

Founded in the 1760s, Sharpsburg was named for Horatio Sharpe, a governor of the colony of Maryland. The town is near the Potomac River on the eastern slopes of the Allegheny Mountains, close to the borders of Pennsylvania and Virginia. To George Washington, who knew the area well, it might have made an excellent location for the new capital of the newly independent United States of America.

In 1790, Congress decreed that the future capital should be located somewhere along the Potomac River. The towns of Shepardstown, Virginia, and Sharpsburg proposed their area as a location for the new capital to President Washington. The president replied with a request for more information on available land in the area. Unfortunately, the people of Shepardstown-Sharpsburg were late in their reply. As a result, in the summer of 1791 Washington and his planners chose another site farther downriver.

To get through Turner's Gap, the Union generals ordered their men to leave the road and advance through the woods. They were to spread out, then hit the Confederates from the flanks. But the rugged, steep terrain slowed the Union advance. As the troops made their way up the hillside, they had to cut their way through dense undergrowth.

When they reached the ridge top, Confederate bullets began to fly. Deadly skirmishes took place between scattered troops who had difficulty seeing their opponents or forming their units into effective firing lines.

Eventually the Union troops forced the Confederate defenders off the top of the mountain. Lee had to order a fighting retreat, but McClellan failed to send reinforcements. The battle wound down in the late afternoon. General Hill withdrew from South Mountain, but the Union forces did not have the numbers to pursue him or maneuver to hit the Confederate troops

CUSTER REPORTS

On the morning of September 15, the day after the Battle of South Mountain, a young staff officer rushed to General McClellan's headquarters. Captain George Armstrong Custer reported that Lee had been wounded in the battle and that Confederate general Hill was dead. Custer also reported a civilian's statement that the Confederate army had suffered 15,000 casualties.[2]

McClellan took this as proof he had won a decisive victory at South Mountain. Unfortunately, all of Custer's information was wrong. Hill was alive, Lee was simply riding in an ambulance, and the Confederate army was still intact. Custer would win a reputation in his own day as a dashing cavalry officer. But he won lasting fame for his miscalculations at the Battle of the Little Bighorn in 1876, when his entire command was wiped out at the hands of Native American warriors.

on the flanks. Instead, the Union troops regrouped on the mountain's western slopes while Lee pulled his main force back to Sharpsburg.

THE EVE OF THE BATTLE

Lee's decision not to retreat to the Potomac after the fighting on South Mountain was extremely risky. If the Union army attacked again before McLaws and Jackson could return from Harpers Ferry, the Confederates would still be seriously outnumbered. Although the Confederates had time to prepare their positions at Sharpsburg, Lee had only a single practical route—the Shepardstown Road to the Potomac—available for retreat.

But Lee knew that if he led his army back across the Potomac, the Maryland campaign would be counted a failure. He would have to fight again in Virginia, his home state, and his troops were already heavily damaged by more than a year of fighting. If he retreated now, he might never have another chance to seize territory in the Union or in the border states.

The Confederate commander also relied on what he knew of McClellan. By this time, the Confederate commander knew McClellan had discovered the Lost Order. He had to assume McClellan knew how Lee had positioned his forces. But even with Lee's own orders in his hands, McClellan was still moving cautiously and failed to pursue Hill's forces retreating from South Mountain. In Lee's

Farms and narrow roads dotted the landscape of the Antietam battlefield.

opinion, it was likely the Union leader would hesitate again before advancing. For these reasons, Lee decided to make his stand at Sharpsburg.

Lee ordered Longstreet to join the Confederate forces assembling east of Sharpsburg, which lay just west of the narrow, winding Antietam Creek. In the meantime, at Harpers Ferry, a bombardment from Confederate guns from Bolivar Heights convinced the Union commander—after holding out for nearly a full day—to raise the white flag.

Stonewall Jackson ordered a forced overnight march on the night of September 15. The next morning his troops arrived, exhausted and bedraggled, to join Lee's army at Sharpsburg. Longstreet's corps also arrived there on September 16 from Hagerstown. The Confederate forces now numbered approximately 350,000.[3]

McClellan brought the Union army up to the woods and hills east of Sharpsburg on September 15. The two armies formed their lines opposite each other in a north–south direction, approximately one mile (1.6 km) apart. Lee pulled his forces closer together in a more compact front. This would allow the Confederate commander to quickly send reinforcements across his line.

The Union army commanded elevated ground east of Antietam Creek. But General McClellan lost the initiative by waiting another day before advancing on the Confederates. Instead of ordering his army forward on September 16, he drew up a detailed battle plan for the next day. The initial assault would take place on the Confederate left, or northern, flank. Stonewall Jackson commanded this sector. After defeating Jackson's troops on the left, McClellan would roll up Lee's line from north to south while keeping the Confederate center and right wing in check.

McClellan issued orders to his corps commanders in isolation, without giving them an idea of the overall objective of the advance and the Union army as a whole. There would be little coordination of action among the divisions along the Union line. In addition, McClellan withheld a large reserve far from the point of attack on his own right flank. While the Union regiments pressed forward

Union sentries used flag signals to send and receive messages between outposts and headquarters.

against stubborn Confederate resistance, more than 20,000 Union troops in these reserve units, about one-third of McClellan's entire force, would spend the entire day watching the battle from a safe distance.[4]

Confederate cannons rained fire down upon Union troops early in the battle.

CHAPTER ★6★

THE DAY OF BATTLE

The bloody Battle of Antietam began in the early morning of September 17, 1862. Two armies—Confederates to the west, Union troops to the east—faced off along a four-mile (6.4 km) front in the hills and valleys of western Maryland. At stake was the Confederate advance into Union-held territory, the fate of Washington, DC, and possibly the final outcome of the Civil War.

By this time, Jackson and McLaws had returned to Sharpsburg from Harpers Ferry. The extra day taken by McClellan to position his troops had given the divided Confederate army time to reinforce and regroup. The two opposing armies were now roughly equal in number. The Union had a larger reserve force, but the Confederates held a shorter, more compact line that would allow Lee to more easily move troops from one end of the field to the other.

McClellan's plan called for an early morning advance along the Hagerstown Pike on the northern end of the battlefield. General Joseph Hooker's I Corps, three divisions strong, marched south along the road, passing two woodlots, known as the East and West Woods, and a large cornfield belonging to a local farmer, David Miller. To Hooker's left, marching through the East Woods in support, was the Union XII Corps, commanded by General Joseph Mansfield.

Confederate guns positioned on Nicodemus Hill, behind the rebel lines, had a clear view of the Union movements. Hidden in the West Woods were rebel troops under Stonewall Jackson's command. As Hooker's troops passed, Jackson's men began firing from the cover of the trees as cannon fire from Nicodemus Hill tore into the Union lines.

There was no retreat and no clear line of escape for Hooker's troops, who were forced to stand and fight. The two opposing lines traded thunderous volleys across a no-man's-land of approximately 100 yards (90 m). In a matter of minutes, hundreds of men from both sides were already lying dead or wounded along the Hagerstown Pike and in Miller's cornfield. Unable to regroup their lines, Jackson's divisions retreated from the road. Their commander was unable to rally them for another assault.

CLARA BARTON

1821–1912

One of the most famous figures to appear at the Battle of Antietam was a Washington, DC, teacher named Clara Barton, nicknamed the "angel of the battlefield." During the Maryland campaign, Barton loaded a wagon full of medical supplies and joined the supply train behind General McClellan's army. On the day of the battle, she drove her wagon forward to the edge of Miller's cornfield just as the battle was dying down there.

Barton brought bandages and other supplies she had gathered to the battlefield surgeons. She offered water, food, and comforting words to the wounded, and she helped the busy surgeons while they amputated limbs and dressed bullet and shrapnel wounds. There was considerable danger. Bullets and shells were still flying at Antietam, and one wounded soldier was shot and killed as Barton crouched by his side.

The aftermath of the battle brought even more work, along with a case of typhus that left Barton sick and delirious. After recovering, she continued her work at the Battle of Fredericksburg, which took place in late 1862. After the Civil War, she set up an office to locate men who went missing during the war, and she helped to establish the American Red Cross in 1881. Barton published her autobiography in 1907 and died in April 1912.

THE ATTACK OF HOOD'S BRIGADE

Suddenly, an elite Texas brigade under General John Bell Hood burst onto the battlefield. Just a few minutes before, these men had been sitting around early morning campfires eating their breakfast. When Hood received the call for assistance from Stonewall Jackson, the Texans left their campfires, took up their rifles, and marched toward the gunfire coming from the Hagerstown Pike. Advancing in line, they fired a volley point blank into Hooker's troops, forcing them back to the shelter of the cornfield.

As the shaken Union troops regrouped at the northern end of the cornfield, Hood's men drew up to face them across ground already blanketed with torn corpses and screaming wounded. For nearly an hour, Hood's brigade fought fiercely, suffering hundreds of casualties. They were outnumbered and could not count on support from other regiments on the Confederate left. Jackson's regiments were now disorganized, with many men fleeing from the fighting.

Although the Confederates had been knocked back, Hooker could not press his advantage. His lines were also under threat from a Confederate brigade under Jubal Early and two more brigades under D. H. Hill, which were maneuvering through the woodlots to hit the Union troops in the flanks. Having already lost 2,500 dead or wounded soldiers, Hooker called for help from General Joseph Mansfield and XII Corps.[1]

Hood's brigade lost nearly half its men during the fighting at Antietam.

A dignified, white-haired gentleman who was admired by the veteran troops under his command, Mansfield ordered his two divisions forward. His mission was to push back the Confederates, secure the Hagerstown Pike, and capture the high ground around a small, square white church, known as the Dunker Church, that lay to the south of Miller's cornfield.

It would be Mansfield's first and last Civil War battlefield experience. Approaching the East Woods, his horse took a crippling shot from the rebel lines. Mansfield dismounted from the wounded animal, intending to stay in the front line with his men. Another fierce volley immediately erupted from the trees. Hit in the abdomen, Mansfield crumpled to the ground. His troops carried him to a nearby field hospital, where he died before midday.

GENERAL SUMNER ARRIVES

As Mansfield was carried from the battlefield, General Alpheus Williams took command of XII Corps. His men fought through the East Woods, pushing Hood's shattered brigade back beyond the cornfield. By this time, Stonewall Jackson's call for reinforcements had reached General Lee, who ordered General John Walker's division—two brigades of North

THE DUNKERS OF SHARPSBURG

A small, square white meeting house lay among the peaceful fields and pastures near Sharpsburg. Locals knew it simply as the Dunker Church, where members of a tiny German religious sect held their observances.

The Dunkers traced their origins to 1708, when their first eight members were baptized. Rather than slipping just their heads or upper bodies into baptismal water, the Dunkers—also known as the German Baptist Brethren—believed in going fully underwater. The Dunkers were a minority sect similar to the Amish or Mennonites who settled along with other German families in western Maryland, Pennsylvania, and the Shenandoah Valley of Virginia. They were pacifists who did not join either Union or Confederate armies. Their meetinghouse at Sharpsburg fell into disrepair in the early 1900s, and it was rebuilt. Although the Dunker sect disbanded in 1962, their meetinghouse stands today as one of the most visited monuments on the Antietam battlefield.

Carolina troops—to march on the double from the Confederate right flank up to the northern part of the battlefield. Walker's men stopped the advance of XII Corps, but Lee was left practically without a reserve force.

McClellan believed his army's best chance for victory was to break through the Confederate center and strike Sharpsburg, where Lee had his headquarters. He ordered General Edwin V. Sumner forward with two full Union divisions. Riding at the head of his troops, Sumner kept them in columns. Column formation allowed units to move quickly along roads, but it could be disastrous if caught by enemy units on a battlefield. After Sumner's lead division passed the southern edge of the East Woods, it turned to face the rebels on the open ground leading to the Dunker Church.

Just as the column emerged from the woods, it was confronted by McLaws's division, which Lee had ordered to the left wing after its arrival from Harpers Ferry. The Confederate troops poured a withering fire into the left flank of Sumner's columns, cutting down hundreds of men in the space of just 15 minutes.

Sumner's troops scattered and retreated. The Confederate generals held their ground, including the Dunker Church. The heavy casualties, shattering artillery fire, and close-up firefights in this part of the battlefield left men on both sides dazed and their units unable to stage any further assaults. Late in the morning, the firing in this sector of the battlefield died away.

The Dunker Church still stands, more than 150 years after the battle.

FIGHT FOR THE SUNKEN ROAD

Confederate troops under General Hill then took up positions in a sunken lane
that zigzagged away from the Hagerstown Pike, approximately one-half mile
(0.8 km) north of Sharpsburg. A split-rail fence ran along the lane; the
Confederate troops had used its wood to build a barrier against the expected
Union advance. The events over the next few hours would make the Sunken Road
at Antietam one of the most famous and terrifying landmarks of the Civil War.

In midmorning, Union troops under General William French came over a small hill 100 yards (90 m) to the west of the lane. A volley from the Confederate line smashed into French's regiments, and many of the survivors broke and fled. Union troops led by General Nathan Kimball then came up as reinforcements, followed by New York's hard-fighting Irish Brigade under General Thomas Francis Meagher.

Union and Confederate troops traded close-range volleys, carpeting the lane and the hillside with bleeding and motionless bodies. As more waves of reinforcements came from the direction of Sharpsburg, the Confederates managed to hold and defend their position through savage hand-to-hand fighting.

THE FIGHTING IRISH

The renowned Irish Brigade of volunteers, forming several regiments of hard-fighting, first-generation immigrants, played an important role in the Civil War. Recruited mainly from New York, Pennsylvania, and Massachusetts, these troops were led by Thomas Francis Meagher, a dedicated supporter of the Union cause. By joining the US Army and fighting the Confederacy, Meagher believed his troops could win acceptance among an American population still largely opposed to Irish immigration.

At Antietam, the Irish Brigade fought on the Sunken Road at midday. The unit proudly carried gold, green, and white battle flags showing a traditional Irish harp and Gaelic text reading "Who Never Retreated from the Clash of Spears." Exposed on the hill before a regiment of North Carolina infantry, the Irishmen engaged in a fierce firefight. More than half of the brigade's men fell dead or wounded by the time the battle ended.[2] The brigade continued to fight in later Civil War battles, sustaining more heavy casualties.

Still, the Confederates, as on the rest of the battlefield, were seriously outnumbered. Sumner's forces numbered more than 15,000 men—an overwhelming force to pour fire on such a short front.[3]

At this point in the battle, confusion reigned on both sides. Artillery shells exploded with a deafening noise as thick smoke drifted across the battlefield. Wounded and frightened men fled in all directions. Commanders were uncertain of their opponents' positions, and couriers were going astray with messages and orders. Given instructions to swing north and repulse any attack coming from that direction, a brigade of Confederate troops mistakenly moved away from the front altogether, creating a wide gap in the Confederate line.

The Union regiments pressed forward into the gap, turning south and opening fire on General Hill's flanks. Confederates defending the sunken land now found themselves vulnerable, defending a death trap. Hundreds of men fell, making it impossible for the survivors to hold the line or maneuver to meet the volleys coming from their left.

Hill's regiments scrambled back toward Sharpsburg as the Union troops advanced into the sunken lane. Many of the blue-coated soldiers tripped and fell, unable to find solid ground between the scores of dead and wounded. Hill sent an urgent message begging Lee for help, but the only reinforcements arriving were several batteries of guns brought up by General Longstreet.

The sunken lane quickly filled with the bodies of fallen soldiers.

Union cannons answered with their own fire at the Confederate position. Shells crashed into the Confederate guns, killing several gunners and touching off explosions of the caissons that carried their ammunition. Realizing that a further Union advance could break through the Confederate center, continue into the streets of Sharpsburg, and threaten Lee's headquarters, Hill rallied a few hundred men for a desperate charge. The assault temporarily stopped the Union troops, who held up between the Sunken Road and Sharpsburg, waiting for further orders.

LATER FAME FOR ANTIETAM VETERANS

When General John Hatch, commander of the Union First Division, I Corps, fell wounded early on September 17, command of his unit was transferred to a career US Army officer from New York, Brigadier General Abner Doubleday. Lasting fame came to Doubleday when a commission set up in the early 1900s to investigate the origins of baseball credited him for inventing the game at Cooperstown, New York, in 1839. Doubleday was an army cadet at the time, however, and never referred to baseball either in his letters or to friends.

Modern historians believe that Doubleday probably had nothing to do with the invention of baseball, although Cooperstown now hosts the Baseball Hall of Fame.

Also serving in the Union army at Antietam was William McKinley, a young sergeant of Company E, Twenty-Third Ohio Infantry, as well as McKinley's regimental commander, Lieutenant Colonel Rutherford B. Hayes. After the Civil War, both men would become US presidents.

General Franklin still commanded 8,000 fresh troops, and he pressed the reluctant Sumner for a renewed advance on the Confederate center. But Sumner outranked Franklin, and when McClellan came out of his headquarters and up to the battlefield to have a look, he agreed with Sumner. Always cautious in the heat of battle, McClellan realized pushing forward without securing the left flank of his army could lead him into a disastrous trap. The Union forces stood their ground, and the fighting in the center of the line began to die down.

Union forces attempted to cross the Rohrbach Bridge against heavy enemy fire.

FIGHTING AT THE ROHRBACH BRIDGE

The Antietam battlefield was a scene of noise, smoke, chaos, and death. The Union and Confederate armies had fought to an exhausted standstill around the Dunker Church and the Sunken Road. Sharpsburg was still in Confederate hands, but McClellan had thousands of men in reserve, ready for the fight. Southeast of the town, along a bend in Antietam Creek, the fighting was only beginning.

On the Union left wing, General Ambrose Burnside commanded IX Corps, four divisions totaling 14,000 men.[1] Although McClellan had ordered these units forward, at first they were not successful in getting across Antietam Creek. Burnside believed his men could cross the stream at this point only by means of a narrow stone bridge, which local farmers knew as the Rohrbach Bridge. The stream was less than 50 feet (15 m) wide at any point. It would have been easy for men and horses to cross slowly through the shallow water, but under enemy fire Burnside insisted upon using the bridge.

Defending the bridge on the opposite side on this day were three regiments of Georgia sharpshooters—only 550 men in all—under the command of General Robert Toombs.[2] The Confederates were positioned on a hilltop overlooking the west end of the bridge. Although they were heavily outnumbered, they poured deadly accurate fire onto the bridge from the heights on the opposite bank. Union troops trying to cross the bridge, or even approaching it, were driven back or shot.

In the meantime, Union scouts had found two crossing locations farther downstream. A division under General Isaac Rodman marched to the first location but discovered steep banks and a high bluff on the opposite side that would have made for a deadly crossing. Rodman's division continued to Snavely's Ford, one-half mile (0.8 km) downstream. Out of the range of Toombs's troops, Rodman led his men safely across Antietam Creek, regrouped his lines, and advanced from the south on the Confederates.

Meanwhile, the IX Corps finally made it across the creek and stormed Toombs's position, forcing the Confederates to retreat toward Lee's headquarters at Sharpsburg. Seeing the blue-coated regiments reforming their lines and approaching, the Confederate artillery batteries around Sharpsburg opened fire from their elevated positions. The best Lee could do was hold off the advance, however. He was now out of reserves and facing the possibility of an all-out assault by Burnside's troops. Union soldiers were pouring across the Rohrbach Bridge and across the fords to the south unopposed.

PANIC IN SHARPSBURG

Burnside's divisions hurried forward, driving the Confederates back. Frightened and wounded Confederate troops began scrambling through the streets of Sharpsburg, while Union shells by the dozen burst in the streets and against homes and shops. Several fires broke out in the town while the Confederate leaders desperately attempted to rally their men for a counterattack. If the Union troops broke through to the west, they would

GENERAL BURNSIDE'S LEGACY

Among Union generals, Ambrose Burnside did not enjoy the fame of George McClellan or the ultimate victory of Ulysses Grant, who would accept General Lee's war-ending surrender in 1865. Burnside experienced both failure and success during the war. At Antietam, confusing orders he issued to his men at the Rohrbach Bridge led to a Union setback and the stalemated position of the opposing armies at the end of the day. Burnside was also largely responsible for one of the worst Union defeats of the war, at the Battle of Fredericksburg in Virginia in December 1862.

Burnside had the support of his staff and his troops, who admired him for his relatively easygoing personality. After the war, he won election as a senator from Rhode Island. The Rohrbach Bridge was renamed Burnside's Bridge in his honor, but he is best known today for the bushy facial hair that lined both sides of his face and inspired the term *sideburns*.

capture the Shepardstown Road—Lee's only means of escape to the Potomac and Virginia.

It was midafternoon and a dangerous moment for the Confederate army. But the battle was not over. Just as Union skirmishers reached the outskirts of Sharpsburg, General A. P. Hill's division of five Confederate brigades appeared on the road from Harpers Ferry. Hill's troops had just finished a hard, hurried, 17-mile (27 km) march from the captured town. Although many of his troops had fallen out of line, Hill managed to bring 3,000 men to the battle.[3] On reaching the battlefield, he ordered his division forward immediately while his officers rallied stragglers to the front line.

Facing Hill on the Union left was a regiment of Connecticut volunteers who had been in uniform for just three weeks. For many of these untested soldiers, Antietam would be their only battle experience. A volley from Hill's brigade slammed into the regiment's line, killing and wounding many of them in an instant. Seeing the enemy in confusion, with scores of terrified men fleeing the battlefield, Hill pressed his attack forward, rolling up Burnside's line and bringing the Union advance on Sharpsburg to a halt.

THE UNION RESERVE

It was now late afternoon. McClellan still held four fresh divisions—approximately 20,000 men—in reserve, roughly one-third of his entire army.[4]

Hill's forces were known as the Light Division.

THE FATEFUL PAROLE AT HARPERS FERRY

The surrender of the Union garrison at Harpers Ferry left more than 12,000 prisoners in Confederate hands—the largest surrender by Union forces during the war.[5] The Southerners could not feed and shelter so many men under guard. The answer was a parole, an ancient military custom in which a prisoner is released on the promise that he will not take up arms again until exchanged for another prisoner.

Handling the parole of the Union troops fell to General A. P. Hill, whose men spent much of the day on September 16 taking names and issuing instructions. The job was not finished until the morning of September 17, when the battle of Antietam had already begun. Hill force-marched his men 17 miles (27 km) to the battlefield, where his regiments managed to stop the Union onslaught on Sharpsburg. The delay was just long enough to keep Hill's men off the battlefield until the closing stages of the battle.

But the Union commander believed Lee had many more men under his command than had appeared in the battle so far. He figured Lee must have been saving thousands of fresh troops in reserve for a surprise assault at the end of the day. The sudden appearance of A. P. Hill and his brigade on the battlefield seemed to confirm his fears.

Several of McClellan's officers were asking to move their units against Sharpsburg. The town and Lee's headquarters were, by this time, in range of the heavy Union guns. But McClellan considered the big picture and proceeded with caution. If a Union attack was repulsed and his Army of the Potomac thrown back or scattered, there was no force between Antietam Creek and Washington, DC, that could stop the

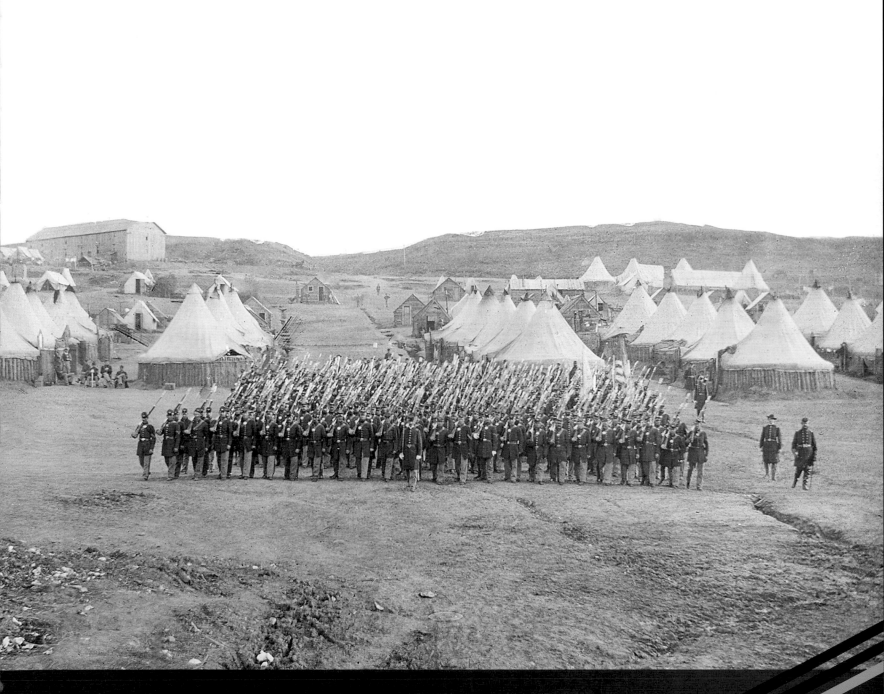

Though McClellan had large reserves of men and equipment, he refused to commit them to the battle.

Confederates. His mission at this point, as he saw it, was to hold his position and convince Lee to retreat.

For that reason, McClellan held his reserve back, waiting for an assault from the Confederate line that never came. Lee managed to hold Sharpsburg. Hill's reinforcements anchored his right flank, Jackson was on the left, and Longstreet's troops and artillery still defended the approaches to the town in the center. These were all the troops Lee had left—there was, in fact, no Confederate reserve available.

Eventually the shots ended and the guns fell silent. The flames sprouting from several homes in Sharpsburg began to die out. The fields to the east of the

STRANGE EXPERIENCES ALONG BLOODY LANE

The Sunken Road lay a few feet beneath the level of the surrounding fields on the Antietam battlefield. In the early afternoon of the battle, Union and Confederate regiments fought a close-range battle over the lane. The heavy firing and hand-to-hand fighting left the path strewn with hundreds of corpses from both sides.

After the war, the Sunken Road was renamed Bloody Lane. Some visitors have claimed to experience an eerie quiet in the vicinity of the lane, as well as voices, singing, battle cries, the smell of gunpowder, and the sight of Confederate soldiers who vanished in the mist. Bloody Lane is just one of several spots, including the Dunker Church, Burnside's Bridge, and McClellan's headquarters at the Pry House, said to be haunted by the ghosts of Antietam.

Longstreet set up effective defenses using his artillery batteries.

town were now littered with the remains of the battle: dead and wounded men and horses, rifles thrown aside, abandoned equipment, tattered regimental flags. Several injured men who had crawled into haystacks for cover had been burned to death as the hay was set alight by bursting shells. Union and Confederate doctors and stretcher-bearers moved to the front with their lanterns to search for the survivors. More than 20,000 dead or injured men were now lying in the once-peaceful valley of Antietam Creek.[6] The deadliest single-day battle of the Civil War was over.

PRESIDENT DAVIS MAKES A BOAST

As the war ground on, the Confederate army called for more volunteers. Leading the effort was President Jefferson Davis, who boasted of phantom victories to inspire Southerners to follow the Confederate flag into battle. At a speech delivered in Jackson, Mississippi, Davis claimed:

> In considering the manner in which the war has been conducted by the enemy, nothing arrests the attention more than the magnitude of the preparations made for our subjugation. Immense navies have been constructed, vast armies have been accumulated, for the purpose of crushing out the rebellion. It has been impossible for us to meet them in equal numbers; nor have we required it. We have often whipped them three to one, and in the eventful battle of Antietam, Lee whipped them four to one. . . . We want public opinion to frown down those who come from the army with sad tales of disaster, and prophecies of evil, and who skulk from the duties they owe their country.[7]

THE NEXT DAY

As dawn broke on September 18, both Confederate and Union armies held their positions around Sharpsburg and Antietam Creek. General McClellan still had two reserve corps ready for battle. Yet he was uncertain of Lee's intentions, and he feared the Confederates were ready to regroup. If he threw the Union army forward and the Confederates put up a strong defense, he might only prolong the stalemate. He issued one order to move forward, but then withdrew it. The Union army waited.

The Confederates had taken thousands of casualties. Lee's situation in western Maryland was precarious. There was little food available. The populace had fled, and local farms had taken heavy damage in the battle. In addition, the expected pro-Confederate uprising in Maryland was not taking place.

The Southerners had only a single line of supply back to Virginia. If a Union force crossed the Potomac to block this route, General Lee's army would be stranded. This convinced Lee to stage a retreat across the Potomac on the night of September 18. His army was battered but still intact. Lee's invasion of Maryland had ended, but the general was not discouraged. He began laying plans for another campaign in Virginia and, eventually, another invasion of the North.

GARDNER'S PICTURES

A few days after the Battle of Antietam, Alexander Gardner arrived at the battlefield with a camera and photographic equipment in a horse-drawn wagon. Walking the fields where burial troops were still digging graves and moving bodies, Gardner took 70 images of Antietam's terrible aftermath.

The photographs showed dead men and horses, broken trees, damaged houses, and a few living men caught from a respectful distance or standing still for the camera. In some cases, Gardner moved bodies into position to enhance the dramatic effect. Gardner took the pictures back to New York, where his employer, Mathew Brady, displayed them as an exhibition for the public. Gardner's images were the first photographs of dead soldiers on a battlefield, and they shocked the public. Although newspapers glorified the war, Gardner revealed the harsh, gruesome reality.

A review in the *New York Times* explained that "Mr. Brady has done something to bring home to us the terrible reality and earnestness of war. . . . If he has not brought bodies and laid them in our door-yards and along streets, he has done something very like it."[8]

Gardner photographed fallen troops along the Hagerstown Pike.

Nearby barns became temporary hospitals following the battle.

THE PROCLAMATION

Antietam was the bloodiest single day in US military history. The battle claimed approximately 23,000 casualties, including approximately 3,650 dead and missing.[1] Infantry fighting and artillery fire destroyed homes and farms near Sharpsburg, and the Confederate invasion had touched a large swath of western Maryland. Pastures and crop fields were damaged in a two-mile (3.2 km) swath along Antietam Creek.

For days, thousands of injured men lay helpless, without food, water, or medical attention. Neither the Union nor the Confederate commanders were willing to collect the wounded under a flag of truce—which, by military custom, was the same as admitting defeat. The temporary shelters set up by military doctors could not handle the flood of wounded men, many of whom would die from infection over the next few weeks and months.

A SURGEON WRITES HOME

For army doctors, the day of battle brought expectation and dread. William Child, a surgeon with the Fifth New Hampshire Volunteers, wrote to his wife describing Antietam:

The days after the battle are a thousand times worse than the day of the battle— and the physical pain is not the greatest pain suffered. How awful it is—you cannot have until you see it any idea of affairs after a battle. The dead appear sickening but they suffer no pain. But the poor wounded mutilated soldiers that yet have life and sensation make a most horrid picture. I pray God may stop such infernal work—though perhaps he has sent it upon us for our sins.[2]

Dr. Child attended to 64 wounded men at Antietam. Later, he would be present at the battles of Fredericksburg, Chancellorsville, and Gettysburg. He also witnessed the assassination of Abraham Lincoln in April 1865.

The fighting at Antietam lasted 12 hours. Despite the prolonged fighting, the battle was not decisive. McClellan's army prevented any further advance by the Confederates into Maryland. By midday on September 19, the Army of Northern Virginia had crossed the Potomac River back into the South. Nevertheless, Lee still commanded a formidable force, and he would not abandon his original objective. He would order another invasion of the North in the summer of 1863. The Confederates would pass over the same ground on their way to Pennsylvania, where they would meet defeat at the Battle of Gettysburg in early July.

General McClellan's failure to pursue Lee into Virginia dashed President Lincoln's hopes for a decisive victory and a Confederate surrender. Instead, the war would drag on until April 1865, with several major battles to come.

Lincoln abandoned any hope of reconciliation with the South and a negotiated truce. He was also aware that a strong faction of Northern Democrats still believed there was nothing immoral or unconstitutional about slavery. This division posed a serious threat to the Union's war effort. Lincoln believed the time had come to take decisive action against slavery.

FREEING THE SLAVES

After McClellan ignored Lincoln's order to pursue Lee into Virginia after Antietam, the correspondence between the two men grew more abrasive and confrontational. Finally, in late October, McClellan began a sluggish crossing of the Potomac, an effort that took him more than nine days. Exasperated, Lincoln finally removed McClellan from his command in November, replacing him with General Burnside.

Nevertheless, the president saw the outcome of Antietam as an important opportunity. He had already prepared an emancipation proclamation, an executive order that would make the end of slavery an official goal of the Union war effort. On the advice of Secretary of State William Seward, he withheld it until the Union could score a military victory. If it seemed the federal

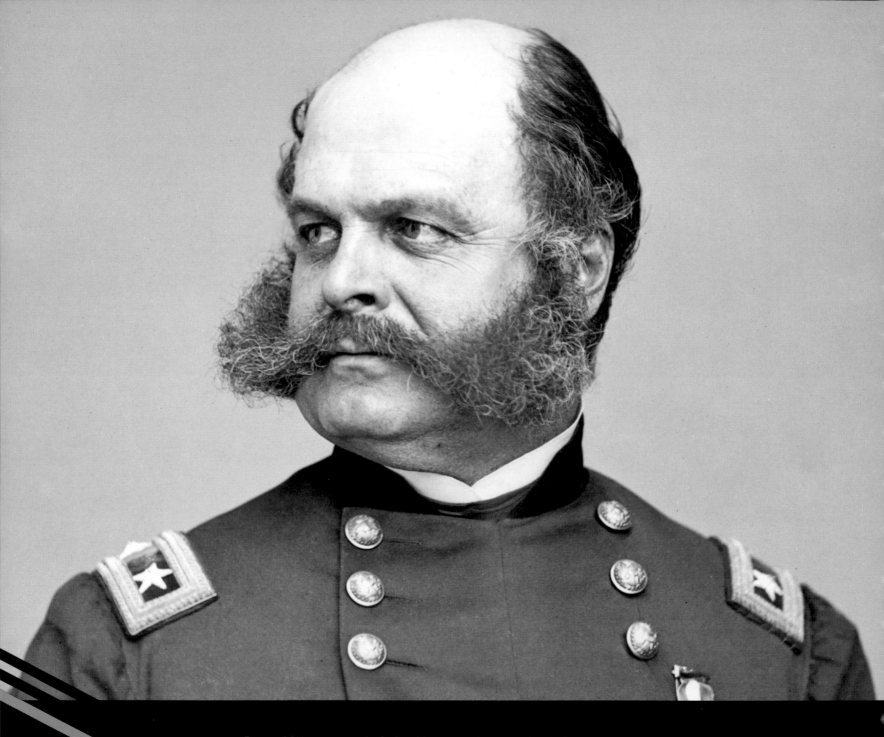

Burnside commanded the IX Corps for much of the war.

government would not be able to enforce emancipation, such a proclamation would appear to the public as an empty gesture.

On the prodding of Abraham Lincoln and abolitionist lawmakers, Congress had already passed new laws on the subject of slavery and emancipation. In April 1862, a new federal law freed all slaves in Washington, DC, and compensated owners $300 for each slave they lost by the law.[3] By acts of Congress passed in July 1862, all slaves that were property of owners in active rebellion against the United States were declared free. This law also authorized the president to recruit freed slaves into the Union armies.

Then the battle of Antietam occurred. On September 22, five days after the battle, Lincoln issued the "preliminary emancipation proclamation." By his authority as commander in chief, Lincoln declared, he now ordered that:

PRESIDENT LINCOLN LAYS DOWN THE LAW

The preliminary emancipation proclamation was just the first of several orders that changed the character of the Civil War. The president also announced that military courts could now try "all Rebels and Insurgents, their aiders and abettors within the United States, and all persons discouraging volunteer enlistments, resisting militia drafts, or guilty of any disloyal practice."[4] Even as slaves won their right to freedom under the Emancipation Proclamation, Lincoln's actions after Antietam imposed the strict authority he believed the Union needed to put down the Southern rebellion.

On the first day of January . . . all persons held as slaves within any State, or designated part of a State, the people whereof shall then be in rebellion against the United States shall be then, thenceforward, and forever free.[5]

The preliminary emancipation proclamation was an ultimatum. In effect, the Confederate government was given three months to come to peace terms. If it did not, Lincoln's proclamation would go into effect, ending slavery by the president's executive authority and abolishing the foundation of the Southern economy.

It did not matter whether a slave belonged to a Southerner who opposed secession or whether the slave owner supported the Union cause. In addition, there would be no compensation to slave owners for the loss of their slaves. All slaves, whether they had escaped or not, would now be welcomed into the Union armed forces—a serious threat to the Confederacy at a time when both sides were struggling to raise new volunteers for the war effort.

THE AFTERMATH OF ANTIETAM

Antietam turned out to be a crucial turning point of the Civil War, both in military and political terms. It ended the Confederate army's invasion of Maryland, an important border state. It boosted Northern morale at a time when the Union had been winning few of its battles, and it removed the possibility of

Lincoln's actions after the Battle of Antietam turned the war into an explicit effort to end slavery in the United States.

European backing of the Confederacy. It also led to the decisive confrontation between McClellan and President Lincoln.

McClellan had won praise in the press for Antietam, but he was also criticized for allowing Lee to escape to Virginia with his army intact. The president waited several weeks for the battle to fade in the public's memory, then dismissed the army's most popular and troublesome leader.

The Emancipation Proclamation was controversial in the North, in the South, in the border states, and overseas. Some criticized it for not going far enough, freeing only the slaves in the Southern states. London newspaper, the *Spectator*, commented, "The principle is not that a human being cannot justly own another, but that he cannot own him unless he is loyal to the United States."[6]

POST-ANTIETAM AMENDMENTS

In December 1865, after the Civil War, the Thirteenth Amendment was ratified, barring slavery throughout the nation. Adopted in 1868, the Fourteenth Amendment made anybody born in the United States a citizen of the country and gave all persons within the United States equal protection under the law. This meant the laws of the states and of the federal government could not treat individuals differently based on their race, color, or creed.

For the people of the Confederacy, the Emancipation Proclamation meant a struggle for survival and a war to the bitter end. The Confederacy was unwilling to give up slavery, and the war would not end as long as slavery survived. The final surrender of General Lee and the Confederate States of America would come only after almost three more years of fighting, in April 1865, and after the deaths of many thousands more soldiers.

TIMELINE

November 1860

Abraham Lincoln wins the popular vote in the 1860 presidential election.

February 9, 1861

The Confederate States of America are established.

April 12, 1861

Confederate shore batteries open fire on Fort Sumter in Charleston Harbor.

April 15, 1861

Lincoln calls for 75,000 volunteers to put down the rebellion.

September 13, 1862

Union soldiers discover Special Order 191.

September 14, 1862

Union and Confederate forces clash at the Battle of South Mountain.

September 17, 1862

An all-day battle occurs along Antietam Creek.

September 22, 1862

Lincoln issues the preliminary emancipation proclamation.

July 21, 1861

The Confederate army wins the Battle of Bull Run, at Manassas, Virginia.

June 25–July 1, 1862

The Union army loses the Seven Days' Battle.

August 28–30, 1862

A Union army is defeated at the Second Battle of Bull Run.

September 4, 1862

Under the command of General Robert E. Lee, the Army of Virginia invades Maryland.

January 1, 1863

The Emancipation Proclamation takes effect.

July 1863

The Confederate army is defeated at the Battle of Gettysburg.

November 8, 1864

Lincoln is reelected as president, defeating George McClellan.

April 9, 1865

Robert E. Lee formally surrenders at Appomattox Court House in Virginia, ending the Civil War.

ESSENTIAL FACTS

KEY PLAYERS

- Abraham Lincoln served as president of the United States during the Civil War, including during the Battle of Antietam.

- General Ambrose Burnside commanded IX Corps during the Battle of Antietam.

- General George B. McClellan commanded the overall Union forces at Antietam.

- General Robert E. Lee commanded the overall Confederate forces at Antietam.

- General Thomas "Stonewall" Jackson commanded a crucial Confederate division at Antietam.

- Jefferson Davis served as president of the Confederate States of America.

CASUALTIES

- Dead: Union: 2,100; Confederate: 1,550

- Wounded: Union: 9,550; Confederate: 7,750

- Missing: Union: 750; Confederate: 1,020

- Total: Union: 12,400; Confederate: 10,220

IMPACT ON WAR

The Battle of Antietam resulted in the retreat of the Army of Northern Virginia, ending the 1862 invasion of Maryland by General Lee's Confederate army. Although General McClellan failed to pursue the Confederates, the Union gained an important advantage. Lincoln leveraged this advantage to issue the preliminary emancipation proclamation.

QUOTE

"The days after the battle are a thousand times worse than the day of the battle—and the physical pain is not the greatest pain suffered. How awful it is—you cannot have until you see it any idea of affairs after a battle. The dead appear sickening but they suffer no pain. But the poor wounded mutilated soldiers that yet have life and sensation make a most horrid picture."

—*Union surgeon William Child*

GLOSSARY

ABOLITIONIST

A person who wants to end slavery.

ARTILLERY

A large gun manned by a crew of operators used to shoot long distances.

BATTERY

A coordinated group of large artillery pieces.

BRIGADE

A military unit made up of several regiments, and in some cases an attached cavalry squad and artillery batteries.

CAISSON

A container for ammunition.

CAVALRY

A military unit consisting of soldiers mounted on horseback.

CORPS

A large military unit consisting of several infantry divisions, in addition to artillery, cavalry, engineers, and supply units.

DIVISION

A military unit consisting of two or three infantry brigades.

EMANCIPATION
The act of freeing an individual or group from slavery.

FLANK
The right or left side of a military formation.

INFANTRY
A group of soldiers trained and armed to fight on foot.

MILITIA
A military force made up of nonprofessional fighters.

NO-MAN'S-LAND
The dangerous, unoccupied territory between two warring armies.

REGIMENT
An army unit typically commanded by a colonel.

SECESSION
The formal withdrawal of one group or region from a political union.

ADDITIONAL RESOURCES

SELECTED BIBLIOGRAPHY

Brewster, Todd. *Lincoln's Gamble: The Tumultuous Six Months that Gave America the Emancipation Proclamation and Changed the Course of the Civil War.* New York: Scribner, 2015. Print.

Slotkin, Richard. *The Long Road to Antietam: How the Civil War Became a Revolution.* New York: Norton, 2012. Print.

Waugh, John C. *Lincoln and McClellan: The Troubled Partnership Between a President and His General.* New York: Palgrave, 2010. Print.

FURTHER READINGS

Cummings, Judy Dodge. *The Emancipation Proclamation.* Minneapolis, MN: Abdo, 2017. Print.

Gindlesperger, James and Suzanne. *So You Think You Know Antietam? The Stories Behind America's Bloodiest Day.* Winston-Salem, NC: John F. Blair, 2012. Print.

Whitman, T. Stephen. *Antietam 1862: Gateway to Emancipation.* Santa Barbara, CA: Praeger, 2012. Print.

WEBSITES

To learn more about Essential Library of the Civil War, visit **booklinks.abdopublishing.com**. These links are routinely monitored and updated to provide the most current information available.

PLACES TO VISIT

Antietam National Battlefield
5831 Dunker Church Road
Sharpsburg, MD 21782
301-432-5124
http://www.nps.gov/anti/index.htm
One of the best-preserved Civil War sites, the Antietam battlefield features both guided and self-guided walking tours, a visitor center, the reconstructed Dunker Church, and the Pry House Field Hospital, containing the National Museum of Civil War Medicine.

US National Archives & Records Administration
700 Pennsylvania Avenue NW
Washington, DC 20408
866-272-6272
http://www.archives.gov
This federal agency displays the original five-page draft of the Emancipation Proclamation, issued by President Lincoln after the Battle of Antietam.

SOURCE NOTES

CHAPTER 1. DUSK AT ANTIETAM CREEK

1. "United States Presidential Election of 1860." *Encyclopaedia Britannica.* Encyclopaedia Britannica, 2016. Web. 14 Jan. 2016.

2. "Compensated Emancipation." *Lehrman Institute.* Lehrman Institute, 2016. Web. 14 Jan. 2016.

3. Ted Widmer. "Lincoln Declares War." *New York Times.* New York Times, 14 Apr. 2011. Web. 14 Jan. 2016.

4. "Secession Rejected in Maryland." *Lehrman Institute.* Lehrman Institute, 2016. Web. 14 Jan. 2016.

5. Kathleen Ernst. *Too Afraid to Cry: Maryland Civilians in the Antietam Campaign.* Mechanicsburg, PA: Stackpole, 2007. Print. 23.

CHAPTER 2. THE CIVIL WAR ERUPTS

1. "A Letter from President Lincoln; Reply to Horace Greeley." *New York Times.* New York Times, 24 Aug. 1862. Web. 14 Jan. 2016.

2. Jefferson Davis. "Confederate States of America— Message to Congress April 29, 1861." *Lillian Goldman Law Library.* Yale Law School, 2008. Web. 14 Jan. 2016.

3. Michael G. Williams. "The Baltimore Riot of 1861." *HistoryNet.* World History Group, 8 Aug. 2011. Web. 14 Jan. 2016.

4. "Constitution of the United States." *National Archives.* National Archives, n.d. Web. 14 Jan. 2016.

5. Michael G. Williams. "The Baltimore Riot of 1861." *HistoryNet.* World History Group, 8 Aug. 2011. Web. 14 Jan. 2016.

6. Shelby Foote. *The Civil War: A Narrative. Volume One: Fort Sumter to Perryville.* New York: Vintage, 1986. Print. 53.

CHAPTER 3. TAKING THE WAR TO MARYLAND

1. "Abraham Lincoln and George B. McClellan." *Lehrman Institute.* Lehrman Institute, 2016. Web. 14 Jan. 2016.

2. James M. McPherson. *Tried by War: Abraham Lincoln as Commander in Chief.* New York: Penguin, 2008. Print. 76.

3. "George B. McClellan." *Freedom: A History of Us.* PBS, n.d. Web. 14 Jan. 2016.

4. "1864 Presidential General Election Results." *US Election Atlas.* US Election Atlas, 2012. Web. 14 Jan. 2016.

5. "Call for 300,000 Volunteers." *Collected Works of Abraham Lincoln.* University of Michigan, n.d. Web. 14 Jan. 2016.

6. "George B. McClellan." *Encyclopedia Virginia.* Encyclopedia Virginia, 4 Mar. 2014. Web. 14 Jan. 2016.

CHAPTER 4. MARCHING TO ANTIETAM

1. Dennis Frye. "September Suspense." *Civil War Trust.* Civil War Trust, 2012. Web. 14 Jan. 2016.

2. "Letters and Diaries of Soldiers and Civilians." *Antietam National Battlefield.* National Park Service, n.d. Web. 14 Jan. 2016.

3. Shelby Foote. *The Civil War: A Narrative. Volume One: Fort Sumter to Perryville.* New York: Vintage, 1986. Print. 664.

4. "General Robert E. Lee's 'Lost Order' No. 191." *Civil War Trust.* Civil War Trust, 2014. Web. 14 Jan. 2016.

SOURCE NOTES
CONTINUED

CHAPTER 5. THE EVE OF ANTIETAM

1. John Keegan. *The American Civil War: A Military History*. New York: Knopf, 2009. Print. 167.

2. Richard Slotkin. *The Long Road to Antietam: How the Civil War Became a Revolution*. New York: Liveright, 2012. Print. 217.

3. D. Scott Hartwig. "The Maryland Campaign of 1862." *Civil War Trust*. Civil War Trust, 2014. Web. 14 Jan. 2016.

4. "The Battle of Antietam: A Turning Point in the Civil War." *Lehrman Institute*. Lehrman Institute, 2016. Web. 14 Jan. 2016.

CHAPTER 6. THE DAY OF BATTLE

1. Shelby Foote. *The Civil War: A Narrative. Volume One: Fort Sumter to Perryville*. New York: Vintage, 1986. Print. 690.

2. Terry L. Jones. "The Fighting Irish Brigade." *New York Times*. New York Times, 11 Dec. 2012. Web. 14 Jan. 2016.

3. "Battle of Antietam." *History Net*. World History Group, 2016. Web. 14 Jan. 2016.

CHAPTER 7. FIGHTING AT THE ROHRBACH BRIDGE

1. Shelby Foote. *The Civil War: A Narrative. Volume One: Fort Sumter to Perryville*. New York: Vintage, 1986. Print. 695.

2. Ibid. 697.

3. Ibid. 699.

4. "Casualties of Battle." *Antietam National Battlefield*. National Park Service, 1 Jan. 2016. Web. 14 Jan. 2016.

5. "Harpers Ferry." *CWSAC Battle Summaries*. National Park Service, n.d. Web. 14 Jan. 2016.

6. "Casualties of Battle." *Antietam National Battlefield*. National Park Service, 1 Jan. 2016. Web. 14 Jan. 2016.

7. "Jefferson Davis' Speech at Jackson, Miss." *The Papers of Jefferson Davis*. Rice University, n.d. Web. 14 Jan. 2016.

8. Heather Murphy. "The Battlefield Photos That Changed Everything." *Slate*. Slate, 17 Sept. 2012. Web. 14 Jan. 2016.

CHAPTER 8. THE PROCLAMATION

1. "Casualties of Battle." *Antietam National Battlefield.* National Park Service, 1 Jan. 2016. Web. 14 Jan. 2016.

2. "Letters and Diaries of Soldiers and Civilians." *Antietam National Battlefield.* National Park Service, n.d. Web. 14 Jan. 2016.

3. Hari Jones. "The Road to Emancipation." *Civil War Trust.* Civil War Trust, 2014. Web. 14 Jan. 2016.

4. James McPherson. *Tried by War: Abraham Lincoln as Commander in Chief.* New York: Penguin, 2008. Print. 132.

5. "Emancipation Proclamation." *National Archives.* National Archives, n.d. Web. 14 Jan. 2016.

6. Amanda Foreman. *A World on Fire: Britain's Crucial Role in the Civil War.* New York: Random, 2010. Print. 318–319.

INDEX

abolitionists, 11, 36, 39, 93
Antietam, Battle of
    Dunker Church, 65, 66, 67, 75, 82
    East Woods, 62, 66–67
    Hagerstown Pike, 62, 64–65, 68
    Miller's cornfield, 62, 63, 64–65, 66
    Rohrbach Bridge, 76–77
    Sunken Road, 68, 69, 70, 72, 75, 82
    West Woods, 62
Antietam Creek, 5, 13, 57, 58, 75, 76, 80, 84–85, 89
Army of Northern Virginia, 5, 23, 90
artillery, 5, 6, 14, 21, 24, 45, 48, 62, 67, 70, 72, 77, 82, 89

Baltimore, Maryland, 10–11, 18, 24–27, 42
Baltimore Riot, 24–27
Barton, Clara, 63
battlefield medicine, 63, 84, 89–90
Brady, Mathew, 86
Brown, George, 26
Brown, John, 47
Bull Run, First Battle of, 31, 32, 33, 36, 40, 41
Bull Run, Second Battle of, 32, 40, 43, 45
Burnside, Ambrose, 34, 75–77, 78, 91

Confederate Army divisions
    A. P. Hill's, 13, 14, 78
    Anderson's, 14
    D. H. Hill's, 14, 48, 54, 55, 64, 68
    Ewell's, 14
    Hood's, 14, 64, 66
    Jackson's, 14, 36, 40, 41, 42, 47, 48, 56–58, 61–62, 64, 82
    Jenkins's, 14
    Jones's, 14
    McLaws's, 14, 47, 48, 53, 56, 61, 67
    Walker's, 14, 47, 48, 66–67
Confederate States of America, 7–9, 10, 19, 29, 97
Custer, George Armstrong, 55

Davis, Jefferson, 23, 24, 29, 36, 84
Democratic Party, 7, 34, 91
Doubleday, Abner, 72

Emancipation Proclamation, 91–97

Fort Sumter, 9, 20–22
Fourteenth Amendment, 96

Gardner, Alexander, 86
Gettysburg, Battle of, 23, 90

Harpers Ferry, Virginia, 46, 47, 48–49, 52, 53, 56, 57, 61, 67, 78, 80
Harrisburg, Pennsylvania, 42
Hayes, Rutherford B., 72
Hicks, Thomas, 12
Hood, John Bell, 64, 66

Irish Brigade, 69

Jackson, Thomas "Stonewall," 36, 40, 41, 42, 47, 48, 56–58, 61–62, 64, 66, 82

Lee, Robert E., 5–6, 13, 22, 23, 36, 39, 40–49, 53–58, 61, 66–67, 70, 72, 76–78, 80, 82–85, 90, 91, 96–97
Lincoln, Abraham, 7, 9, 10, 17, 18, 22, 26–27, 29, 31, 35, 42, 90–91
    relationship with McClellan, 31–33, 34, 35, 96
    views on slavery, 7–9, 18–19, 20, 91–93

Mansfield, Joseph, 62, 64–66
Maryland, 5, 10–11, 14–15, 17, 23, 30, 36, 43, 46, 54, 61, 66, 94
McClellan, George B., 6, 13, 31–35, 39–41, 43–45, 49, 51–56, 58–59, 61–62, 67, 73, 75, 80, 82, 85, 90–91, 96
McDowell, Irvin, 31, 44–45
McKinley, William, 72
Meagher, Thomas Francis, 69
Mexican-American War, 20, 23, 44

New York City, New York, 17

Philadelphia, Pennsylvania, 17–18, 34
photography, 86
Pope, John, 36, 39–40, 43
Potomac River, 6, 11, 30–31, 33, 34, 35–36, 40, 45–47, 52, 54, 56, 78, 80, 85, 90–91

Republican Party, 7, 10, 29, 34
Richmond, Virginia, 29, 30, 33, 35, 39, 40, 43
Rodman, Isaac, 76

Scott, Winfield, 20, 22, 32, 41, 44–45, 47
Seven Days' Battle, 35, 36, 39
Sharpsburg, Maryland, 5, 6, 11, 13, 32, 54, 56–58, 61, 67–70, 72, 75, 77–78, 80, 82, 85, 89
slavery, 7–11, 17–19, 20, 24, 29, 32–33, 36, 39–40, 42, 47, 91–93, 94, 96–97
South Mountain, Battle of, 51–56
Special Order 191, 48–49, 51
Sumner, Edwin V., 67, 70, 73

Thirteenth Amendment, 96
Toombs, Robert, 76

Union army corps
  I Corps, 14, 52, 62, 72
  II Corps, 14
  IV Corps, 14
  VI Corps, 14, 52–53
  IX Corps, 13, 14, 52, 75, 76
  XII Corps, 14, 62, 64, 66–67

Virginia, 6, 11, 17, 22, 23, 30–33, 36, 39, 42, 46, 54, 56, 77, 85, 90, 96

Washington, DC, 6, 10, 17, 18, 29, 33, 36, 39, 40, 42, 45, 52, 61, 63, 80, 93
Williams, Alpheus, 66

ABOUT THE AUTHOR

Tom Streissguth is the author of more than 100 books of nonfiction for the school and library market and the founder of The Archive of American Journalism, a unique collection of historical journalism that is presenting long-neglected work of major American authors including Jack London, Stephen Crane, Lincoln Steffens, Nellie Bly, and Ambrose Bierce. He currently lives in Woodbury, Minnesota.